Why My J.O.B. Quit Me!

Jump-start YOUR Firing

By Mechiel Kopaska,
Project Management Professional,
Real Estate Innovator

Why My J.O.B. Quit Me!
Jump-start YOUR Firing

Published by Kopaska Publishing
P.O. Box 844
Odessa FL 33556

ISBN: 978-0-578-78565-3

Cover design by Jim Saurbaugh

DISCLAIMER AND/OR LEGAL NOTICES
While the publisher and author have used their best efforts in preparing this book, they make no representations or warranties with respect to the accuracy or completeness of the contents of this book. The advice and strategies contained herein may not be suitable for your situation. You should consult a professional where appropriate. Neither the publisher nor the author shall be liable for any loss of profit or any other commercial damages, including but not limited to special, incidental, consequential, or other damages. The purchaser or reader of this publication assumes responsibility for the use of these materials and information. Adherence to all applicable laws and regulations, both advertising and all other aspects of doing business in the United States or any other jurisdiction, is the sole responsibility of the purchaser or reader.

This book is intended to provide accurate information with regard to the subject matter covered. However, the author and the publisher accept no responsibility for inaccuracies or omissions, and the author and publisher specifically disclaim any liability, loss, or risk, whether personal, financial, or otherwise, that is incurred as a consequence, directly or indirectly, from the use and/or application of any of the contents of this book.

To my dad – "Gone missing."

Acknowledgments:

To my sister, Melissa Kopaska for the countless hours we spent on the phone talking about Dad and Grandpa and sharing all the stories and agreeing to what content would fit best and sound good.

To my aunt, Andrea Brubaker for filling in details that I couldn't or didn't remember about Dad and Grandpa.

I'm very thankful and I hope you both find enjoyment and are able to connect with the content.

Table of Contents

Foreword

Success is rarely a straight line for anyone of us. This book will take you on a veritable journey through the personal and professional life of my dear friend and colleague – Mechiel Kopaska. We met over 20 years ago doing our J.O.B.s (you will understand this reference as the book unfolds) as consultants, and I knew then she was unique and more thoughtful than many professionals I encountered at that point in my career. Through the years, we have shared our hopes, dreams, and successes as well as the agony of defeat and personal setbacks. I am fortunate to be considered one of the selected mentors in her life. Mechiel's decision to write this book brought joy to my heart because I have always felt she had meaningful things to say in a truly unique voice.

When Mechiel asked me to pen this foreword, my first reaction was feeling honored and humbled that she would ask me. I then wondered how I might do this book – as well her – the necessary justice they each deserve. As a new author of the first of what I believe will be many books, Mechiel inspires and motivates the reader through relatable experiences that we can appreciate and more importantly… understand. The more I offer advice to clients and executives, the more I realize that the most influential information is delivered in the way you will find in the following chapters… through life experience.

Practical, informative, and entertaining while providing colorful perspective best describe what you will find along Mechiel's journey. For example: Introducing "Failure" as an option – and providing yourself the freedom to fail, while painful and scary – empowers you to explore, grow, and learn in ways you never thought possible. We all as human beings spend inordinate amounts of time considering what others may think about what we do or what we may say, and Mechiel deftly covers letting go of this consideration and why it makes sense and will benefit you in business and your personal life. Thoughtful, provocative, and, at times, raw – you will be inspired in ways you may have never thought possible.

Mechiel takes the "cliché" out of "hard work and perseverance" and makes you feel real through authentic family life growing up in rural America. Her personal triumphs and setbacks have created who she is each and every day; her drive and determination originate from places we all can identify with, appreciate, and aspire to.

An American story with all the trimmings and a healthy dose of "common sense." Thank you for the window into your personal experiences and continuing to challenge all of us and the ways we choose to live.

Thanks Mechiel for sharing your journey and may the wind remain in your face! 😊

Edward A. Schnur

Preface
Bucket Time

It was a fall day in 2004, just after the harvest in Iowa, when I opened the garage door and found my dad sitting on an overturned large white bucket – his elbows on his knees, simply staring at a car frame with an engine.

I approached, "Hey Dad, what are you doing?"

He sat in silence for what seemed like several minutes without blinking, without moving a muscle. I knew better than to prod or interrupt because the consequence of that or turning back to leave him alone would not lead to the right outcome. So I stood in silence too, watching as he puckered his bottom lip and continued to stare at the car frame. I silently recalled that this very car frame sat in our pasture for 23 years, and I knew that because I had mowed around it for all that time.

However, little did I know my dad would turn it into a project during the winter. He'd collected body parts, trim, tires, and seats from all over the country. My sister, Melissa and I were with him when he obtained the trim in Arkansas. The tires came from Goodyear in Florida, and the chrome came from Orlando. I'm not sure where the engine came from, but I didn't need to know.

What I do know is that my father always had an innovative and forward-thinking mind. He was the ultimate problem solver, so much so that I can't tell you how many people would swing by his garage to pick his brain about their own problems. Never a day went by without someone stopping in to see him. Dad was unique in so many ways that I would not come to understand the depth of his skills and insights until many years later. He was a father, husband, brother, uncle, son, and friend to many, but his underlying passion for life made him stand out. There's nothing he couldn't do. Of course, you'd expect me to say that because he was my dad, but I assure you that many, many others would confirm my statement. He touched people everywhere he went from Alaska to Florida, and especially in the Midwest – Iowa and Arkansas. He never met a stranger, and his love language was quality time. Dad never stopped learning.

So why is this important enough to take a tangent away from the story in the garage? It's simple: The environment in which I was raised has everything to do with who I became and my future self. While I watched and absorbed the things Dad did, it wasn't until much later in my life that I truly came to understand my choices and why I made the decisions I did. Those things occurred because of the foundation I had on which I could build my life.

For example, I'll never forget the day when I went home to Iowa and said, "Dad, I think you made me too strong!"

His reply: "No, Shell, I gave you the tools and you did with them what you wanted."

The light bulb went on; he was right.

Back in the garage that day, he was simply staring at a frame. When his timing was right, he tilted his head and gave me a slanted-eye look and simply said two words: "Bucket time."

Bucket time? What on earth does that even mean? I knew better than to ask and knew that Dad loved to give mysterious answers... to make you think. He then went on to explain what he was working on, and I pretended to understand all the mechanics of a 454 big block engine. I simply nodded and trusted him because I knew what he said was real or would become real. I visited a few more minutes and left him to his thoughts and efforts.

Years later, in 2007, on another visit home to Iowa, Dad said, "Hey Shell, come down to the garage." He opened the big door and presented to me and Melissa his prize creation: a fully restored, eye-catching red 1961 Chevy Bel Air... complete with that 454 big block engine, 6-speed manual transmission. That engine thumped as he backed the car out of the garage. The red car contrasted beautifully against the bright green hillside, and he asked me to take plenty of pictures. I mailed enlarged framed pictures back to him.

Two months later, my dad was gone. He'd finished this project just before he'd passed. However, that's not really the moral of the story.

When I recall this event and "bucket time," I realize there were several lessons inside this single story. For me, bucket time is a method of deep concentration to reach the desired result. Thoughts are really powerful tools, and dreams can become reality when you're willing to put in the effort needed. In thinking about my own life, I realize how much bucket time has recently impacted me.

For several years, I was an IT project manager for accounting implementations. It involved a lot of technical and thinking work. Every day led to issues to solve, some of which required extended thinking. I learned that when I got quiet – and specifically carved out time for that – is when I could solve problems. I learned what a valuable tool bucket time is... as valuable as the rest of the tools in my father's garage. Now I intentionally sit in silence to see if I can solve problems and achieve the results I want. I know this practice has made me stronger today, and it is why I decided to write this book – to help you achieve what you want and get the outcomes you desire by employing your own version of bucket time and the other things we'll cover in the pages to come.

As we get started, can you look back on your own upbringing and see your foundational strengths... and weaknesses? What is it that has perhaps impacted your life where you can sit in silence – call it meditation or "me time" if you'd like – to move toward achieving what you want?

If you haven't yet developed the habit of sitting quietly, at least for a few minutes a day, I encourage you to start doing so. Of course, there are plenty of excuses to forego this practice, and I know how hectic, busy, and downright crazy the real estate business can be, and that's also true for every entrepreneur, no matter the industry. However, don't let that be an excuse. The first lesson to share is that setting aside 10 to 15 minutes a day for "bucket time" will always be time well invested. Whatever you call it, start by getting quiet with yourself, and you might just find exactly what you're looking for.

Preface

Chapter One:

Getting Quiet on the J.O.B.

Your brain is incredibly powerful… if you allow it to be. Like my dad sitting on the bucket letting the quiet surround him so his brain could unravel the challenge of re-assembling an engine, there is almost always the best solution to any problem found when you get quiet.

I'll share another story that underscores the power of getting quiet to achieve success. I was assigned to a project in which my company had been hired to implement an accounting solution, and this particular job had its challenges. The team, with one exception, consisted entirely of women. The lone man was my counterpart as the internal project manager while I was the project manager on the vendor side, and we both reported to the CFO who was one tough cookie.

My lead consultant came to me and told me we had an internal saboteur, explaining that someone on the client's side was entering bad data into the system that was then causing the system to fail. Of course, we'd have to prove it, and I needed data to support the accusation before approaching Cynthia, the CFO. A day later he delivered a report that identified the person by log in, the time at which she'd logged in, and the databases she was hitting. We didn't know the exact data she was loading, but test scripts revealed the inaccuracy of the data. We also suspected her motivation.

Faced with this challenge, I called my home office regarding suggestions for proceeding. My boss pretty much curled up in a corner, put the ball back in my court, and said,

"Mechiel, you can do it." For three days, I fretted over what and how I was going to tell the CFO about an internal saboteur. I knew that I had to handle this correctly. After three days of spending some dedicated quiet time, I decided to schedule a meeting and simply tell her everything – honestly and truthfully with reports in hand.

"Cynthia, I don't know a better way to explain this to you other than to be straight and tell you that you have an internal saboteur on your project. Here's the data, and I can prove it."

When I handed over the reports, she stood up from the desk and said, "I was wondering, Mechiel, how long it was going to take you to tell me that?" She already knew and was impressed with the fact that I stood up and presented what I'd discovered in the professional way in which I handled it. Had I not given myself time to get quiet and really think about my approach and my delivery, I doubt I would have gotten the same end result – a happy

> *When you get quiet, you can allow your brain to work for you, rather than letting worrisome, errants thoughts to run amok.*

client who was proceeding with my company's product. In fact, the following day, the HR director was fired. She actually wanted a different product and had high hopes that by destroying the data in our system, it would fail and with failure, the company would revert back to her preferred product.

Ssshhhh....

Now that you are starting to get a glimpse of the importance of quiet time to let your brain work for you rather than having errant thoughts working against you, let's look at a few ways in which you can create your own quiet time. Here are four different things I do to get quiet.

One thing that can be very helpful is to change your scenery. Sometimes when I want quiet time, I'll take a book and my journal and hit the road... literally. I drive to a park or somewhere similar. I may sit there for an hour, doing some reading, internalizing my thoughts, and releasing things. I'll also write in my journal, just letting words flow without worrying too much about them. There's been much written (no pun intended) about the power of journaling and I often find that solutions flow from my pen to the page after a few pages of writing. For me, I have to get away from my typical surroundings. And here's a very important aspect of this exercise: I shut my phone off, so I can really disengage with the world. The inundation of contact and 24/7 accessibility via smart phones can be a huge stressor and an even bigger distraction. You may not believe that and may twitch at the idea of turning off your phone. However, you'll never achieve quiet time for yourself with the dings, beeps, and other audible indicators nagging for your attention.

Working in real estate these days makes for action-packed and very busy days, and it is challenging to make the time to get quiet during the day. This is when I set aside some time in the evenings to sit back and do some deep thinking. You may have a similar daily schedule and will find that evenings (when kids are in bed and things are winding down) to be the best time for you to schedule your quiet time. For some, the end of the day – early in the morning before others are awake – works best. I also journal during this time and spend some time reading as well. While I've mentioned reading in both of the suggestions I've covered so far, I'm not reading novels. My book choices always come from the self-help, inspirational, or spiritual sections of the library, book store, or Amazon genre. I want to read something that offers me something beyond entertainment. I read to gain knowledge and always have to be learning. I read to be inspired.

The third thing that I do that helps me achieve quiet time is to work out. I work out three to four times a week, and before I go to the gym, I'll listen to a podcast (e.g., Robert Kiyosaki, Darren Hardy, Pastor Steven Furtick, Pastor Rick Warren, Tyler Sheff of the Cashflow Guys, and Larry Harbolt – The Real Deal). The combination of the information I just heard and learned and working out makes for a powerful mixture for both mind and body. I suggest you find what triggers you, what makes you who you are, and what you want to learn. Depending on your preferred exercise, you can combine them – listening while walking or running, for example.

The next suggestion I have may seem a little "out there"; however, I ride a motorcycle, and I can assure you that when I'm riding, there's a lot of thinking that goes on. A lot of it is reminiscing and mentally thanking my father for teaching me to ride as well as everything else he taught me. That said, it's also about what I call "wind therapy," going up and down hills and feeling the breeze. Now you may not ride a motorcycle, but there's probably something you do that will have a similar effect – playing a sport, riding a bicycle, running, even walking in the woods. Find something that you find exhilarating that gets you away and by yourself so you can spend some time inside your own head.

I've mentioned that I journal, and as I mentioned, there are numerous studies that support the benefit of this habit and it even goes beyond the benefits to your thought processes. University of Texas at Austin psychologist James Pennebaker "contends that regular journaling strengthens immune cells, called T-lymphocytes" (as quoted on the *PsychCentral* site by Maud Purcell, LCSW, CEAP, "The Health Benefits of Journaling"). Additionally other research suggests journaling decreases the symptoms of asthma and rheumatoid arthritis. Journaling is a stress-management tool, but the effort must go beyond a few sentences or snippets. By writing, you'll access your left brain, and when your analytical left brain is occupied, it frees up your creative right brain to solve problems. Use your specified quiet time to write for about 20 minutes a day, and don't worry about what you write. Just start writing, and like I said, the words will begin to flow and your creative problem solving often appears on the paper in front of you. Your journal is for you to access your thoughts and begin to know yourself better. It's all about driving much needed introspection. Don't write in such a way that you worry about what others may think if they read it. It's yours and it's private.

Grandpa's Dreams

This is actually an extension of bucket time and getting quiet. My grandfather, Arnold Kopaska was born in 1911 and grew up during the Great Depression. Grandpa only had a seventh-grade education because he was pulled out of school at that age to help on the farm to provide for the family. This was actually quite typical during the '30s and in agrarian communities. As a boy, he invented the horse-drawn harrow with a seat – his first invention. Originally, these carts were designed in such a way that the farmer would walk behind them. As Grandpa was quoted, "See, them carts didn't have no seats and I was barefooted, and my feet got so sore I put on a seat so I could ride." He recalled that by about two years later, every farmer had them and put seats on them like he had. (See the link in the Resource section at the end for the full article.)

Unlike my father, Grandpa didn't have a lot of friends and was somewhat egotistical and stingy – a personality that developed based on his upbringing and out of necessity based on the economy during his formative years. At age 50, he invented what became patented as the Rotary Baler, known today simply as the round hay baler. His ideas and inventions were the product of dreams he'd have during the night. He'd go to bed at 6:00 in the evening and be awakened at 2:00 or 3:00 in the morning by a dream. He'd get up and go to the garage and would begin hand-crafting whatever it was that he'd dreampt about, right down to every nut and bolt that he saw in his mind and where they'd go and how the whole thing would go together and work. I was very grateful for Grandpa's dreams and inventions. You see, it was my job at 5:00 in the morning during cold Iowa winters to feed the cows, pitching hay into them twice a day. With the round hay baler, which you'll still see sitting in farm fields today, it sat in the pasture with the cows, so they could feed themselves. I was happy not to have that chore any longer.

My Grandpa and Dad when Grandpa won the Iowa Inventor of the Year award, Nov. 6, 1987.

Now the moral of the story is the ability to let your mind work for you. In both the case of my father and grandfather, they would get quiet in their thinking. My father had bucket time, but for my grandfather, his mind was more creative while he slept – a trait I seemed to have inherited as well. I also have a brain that tends to solve problems while I sleep, and I wake up with the answer.

You may think that sounds far-fetched, but there are plenty of successful entrepreneurs who will attest to the same thing, thinking about the problem as they go to sleep and allowing their brains to sort through all of those cortical folds to find the solution.

Think about how your own brain works and determine when you typically solve problems and are most creative. You may not have the benefit of a brain that is an overnight problem solver, but I am certain that you know when you are most alert during the day and "firing on all pistons." This is when you should be setting aside time to get quiet and capture your brain at its finest.

Consider This...

Pastor Steven Furtick has said:

The voice you believe will determine the future you experience.

If we compare that to what my father did sitting on a bucket and what my grandfather did through his dreams, it's an example of two men believing their own voices. Depending on what you believe, it could have been God speaking to them or a "gut" instinct that led them to believe in what they were doing. Considering the second half of the quote, both men created things out of their imaginations – out of thin air, if you will. My dad created a car from pieces and my grandfather invented and improved farm machinery.

This is relevant in today's society and in your own life. What voice do you believe? Is the voice in your head positive and encouraging... or is it one telling you what you can't do? Stated another way: Whether you believe you can or can't... you're right!

It is truly time to believe in yourself and in your own worth. If you don't take the time to get quiet and let your mind go, you cannot know what the future holds, and you'll fail to tap and explode your own potential.

Getting Quiet on the J.O.B.

Chapter Two:

Fearless

Building on getting quiet, achievement and success also result from being fearless. Now you may not consider yourself fearless today, but you have it within you to "fear less" and by starting to fear less, you are taking the steps you need to ultimately become fearless.

I was really lucky growing up with my father. He NEVER showed fear. There's certainly a possibility that he felt it at times, but I never saw him struggle with finances nor to make decisions. He led by example, tackling everything as it came along. There was nothing he wouldn't try or do to get the outcome he wanted.

My dad owned and piloted a small plane and built his own runway on the farm – too short, in reality, with electrical lines at one end and a river at the other. He didn't give himself room for error; it would lead to possible electrocution or drowning. Once a month on a Sunday, we'd participate in "flight breakfasts." We'd all pile in the plane with my sisters and me in the back and my mom in the co-pilot's seat and fly to a neighboring town. The pancake breakfast was free for everyone who arrived by plane.

The trip back home was always interesting as my dad would practice maneuvers, effectively stunts. Occasionally he'd do what's called a Hammerhead, flying straight up, bleeding off air speed and creating a stall, then dipping the nose downward to restart the engine. Other times, he'd simply shut the engine off and we'd glide for a bit before he re-started it. He'd also make sharp right and left turns, which, having just eaten pancakes didn't always pan out so well, especially for my mom who then opted out of the flight breakfasts.

As kids, it scared the living daylights out of us, but we learned to trust him, and now, looking back as an adult, I understand he was practicing not only to keep his license but to always be prepared for an emergency. I always looked forward to flying, and there were times he even let me take the yoke and fly with him explaining the workings of aeronautics and the various instruments.

Years later, he sold the plane and purchased an ultralight – a one-man set of wings with a seat, a propeller, and small engine. Admittedly, I was bothered by his choice to fly the ultralight as he always looked so small and vulnerable in the sky, and I got a call one day from him telling me that he "fell out of the sky." He wasn't sure what went wrong, but the plane lost pressure and dropped from about treetop height... and those Iowa trees grow pretty tall. Thankfully, he wasn't badly injured and suggested he was done flying; however, years later, when I visited, I saw the cloth ultralight wings in the garage. When I asked him about it, he said he was "just putting it back together." He passed before he was able to take to the skies again.

> *"If we all worked on the assumption that what is accepted as true is really true, there would be little hope of advance."*
>
> ~ Orville Wright

With that role model – my dad who seemed to always tempt fate, I also grew up being somewhat fearless. My grandfather had set the example for my father as well with his inventions… always trying things but without any guarantee that they'd work. It's been suggested that had the Wright brothers attended college, they would have been taught that flight is impossible. Instead, they went to work studying aeronautics, experimenting, and ultimately took the first flight.

Riding Lessons

Like most kids, I wished for a horse when I was growing up. Despite living on a farm, every Christmas morning came and went without me finding a horse in our barn. Although I didn't get my wished-for horse, when I turned nine, I did get a motorcycle for Christmas – a Honda XL 75. Sure, I'd still have preferred the horse, but this was pretty cool. My dad gave me pointers on how to ride but there was much hands-on learning while riding, and after a lot of practice on the farm, he gave me a daily chore that may have been his ultimate motive for giving me the motorcycle in the first place. Now I had to check the cows, and that involved riding over a mile to the pasture to check the cows, count the cows and calves, ensure ear tags were in place, and then ride the fence line to ensure all the fencing was in place and secure.

We actually took family vacations via motorcycles, with my sisters riding with my dad, and me riding with my mom. Dad mounted foot pegs below the gas tank, strapped a pillow on the gas tank with a bungy cord, and this is where Melissa would ride. My other sister sat behind Dad, like normal. This was in the '70s when bikers weren't "cool." People would gawk at us and even flash nasty gestures, associating us with a far more badass crowd than we were. A real lesson in not making snap judgments.

When I turned 16, I got my motorcycle license and graduated to riding my mom's much bigger Honda 500. I'd pick up my girlfriend, Sheila and we'd cruise the downtown, known as "scooping the loop." We probably looked goofy as hell in our helmets, but it was fun. I continued to maintain my license through adulthood, finally culminating in purchasing my first Harley Davidson® Low Rider®. Despite not having ridden for a few years, the memory came back quickly. Soon, I graduated to a Harley Davidson® Street Glide®. For the past 15 years, I've sponsored an annual "Mystery Ride," that starts and ends on my farm outside Tampa during which I map out an interesting 150-mile ride that's followed by a barbeque, music, and bonfire.

As with riding a motorcycle, you must always evaluate risk, and you may find that sometimes that is not always enough. As an example, one day, risk found *me*. Another biker, yes, you're reading this right, another biker took me out! Came up on my right side and completely disintegrated my right saddle bag. By the grace of God, I remained upright. I did go to the ditch and dumped my bike just so I could evaluate others who had been injured. Talk about an adrenaline rush! The good news: I wasn't initially hurt and my bike

> *The secret of life is to fall seven times and get up eight times.*

suffered several thousands of dollars of damage, but that idiot wasn't going to deter me from doing something I loved! I got my bike fixed, and I was back to riding!

One of the best lessons that I ever got from riding and that you can apply in your own quest to become more fearless, is to get back on the proverbial horse when you fall off. Never allow yourself to brew on things that go wrong for too long. Take only as much time as needed to do a quick assessment of why you failed and apply the lesson to avoid the same mistake in the future. If you mull over failure for too long, you let the fear of "falling off again" grow disproportionately and potentially to the point of being too fearful to get back on and ride again, figuratively if not literally.

Life Lessons

When I went to college, leaving the farm in Iowa and heading to Kansas City, my dad and I packed the horse trailer with what little furniture I had and made the trek to the apartment where I'd be living. After unloading, I went back out to double check that I had everything to find that my father had vanished – no good-bye, just gone. It was pretty gut-wrenching being alone in a big city having spent my life on a farm. I didn't know anyone. I only knew two things: how to get to school and my schedule. There wasn't much time to wallow in fear because there were things I had to do. Maybe that was the lesson about being fearless that my father wanted me to learn in that very moment. It was a lot like getting right back on the horse and moving forward.

I made up my mind that I'd simply figure it all out as I went and get it done, and that included finding a job to support myself when I'd never had a job before. Farm chores had been my job to that point. It all was a huge change for me, but between commuting to school, classes, studying, and working at Pizza Hut, I didn't have time to worry, be scared, or even think about fear.

> **"Doubt and fear steal more dreams than failure does."**
> **~ Darren Hardy**

When you create your own plan of action for attempting anything, simply stay focused on the steps you need to take to generate your desired outcome. You'll leave yourself little time for worry and growing fearful, and worry is a waste of your precious time. Consider these steps to overcome worry and ultimately fear:

First, simply do your best. It's all anyone can ask of you, and it's all you can expect of yourself. Stop worrying about what you cannot do. If you find yourself facing something for which you don't have the needed skill, figure out how to learn it, learn it, and apply it rather than taking time to worry that you can't do something or that you currently lack the skill. I assure you, my grandfather never worried about the possibility of his inventions not working. Sometimes they didn't work as expected, so that simply meant it was back to the drawing board. Like him, I've never been afraid to give something a try. In fact, when someone tells me I can't do something, that is all I need to hear to do it… just to prove a point. I once had a boss who told me I was a computer whiz but didn't know math. Math wasn't part of my college course of study, so I signed up for an algebra class to prove to him I could do it, took the college-level course, and slapped my "A" on his desk. Adopt that attitude. Remove fear from your life and you can do anything. Don't think about it or waste mental energy on worry. Just do it.

Remove the word fear from your personal vocabulary. Don't say you're afraid of something. Instead, admit that you aren't sure how things might go and what the outcome might be but that you're willing to give it a try and learn as you go. Simply evaluate: "What's the worst that can happen?" Avoid letting fear become your dance partner and just make a move, any move, instead. Hand in hand with that, stop caring what others think. Rather than moving with the herd, be the exception and do your own thing. You'll find that you'll very likely become a role model for others. Anyone who's ever accomplished anything has had to stand out and choose a path other than the one well-worn by the herd.

Stop worrying about what *might* happen. Yes, things go wrong, so expect the unexpected. That was exactly what my father was doing in the plane when we thought he was simply doing stunts. In much the same way that things go wrong, mistakes are also inevitable. Accept that you are going to make 'em and that in doing so, you are perfectly normal. *The worst mistake you can make is to waste time and mental energy worrying that you are going to make a mistake.* Ditto to uncertainty. There will always be uncertainties. Don't worry; instead embrace what's new and that something exciting is right around the corner for you.

Believe in your own skill set. When I was fired, it was actually a relief. Sound crazy? I was relieved because first and foremost, I believed in my own skill set and I knew what I had to offer another company and, in fact, the world. And with that, I launched my own consulting company. A huge stepping stone in becoming fearless is to believe in who you are and what you have to offer. Believe in your own knowledge and experience. You'll find that belief in yourself and worry cannot coexist.

Visualize things going right. There is much written on the power of positive thinking. Your thoughts affect your actions, and your actions affect your outcomes. Your mindset truly matters, and there is incredible power in positive thinking. The first step is yours to take in that direction. That on which you fixate tends to always come your way. Focus on what you want, not on what you don't want.

Never Say Never

When I was getting ready to leave home, my dad asked me what I wanted to do in my life. I told him that I wanted to collect as many license plates as I could by living in different states. However, I also told him that I would never live "out east." Growing up in Iowa, there aren't a whole lot of people, and I knew that out east, there was a lot of congestion because it was (and is) far more densely populated. Big cities and a fast pace. Admittedly, the thought intimidated me.

As luck would have it, upon graduation, I returned to Iowa and took a job with Greyhound in the travel department. I did a good job and they approached me with a promotion: to a much bigger office… in Philadelphia. For me, that was about as "out east" as it got. Intimidating though it seemed, I decided it was in my best interest to give it a shot. Maybe the city

> **"Don't let the fear of losing be greater than your excitement of winning."**
> **~ Robert Kiyosaki**

wasn't as intimidating as I'd imagined, and I recalled how my father dropped me off in Kansas City and literally left me on my own and to my own devices. This time, he traveled with me and stayed for three days. I was without a car and living in a hotel for two and a half months at 10th and Race Street. My commute was only two blocks on foot.

When I look back on it, I'm a little shocked that I did it because I was so determined that out east would not be for me. I knew nothing of city living and was now in the dead heart of a major city. As a country girl who went to the city in 1986, I was unaware of how unsafe some situations were or could be. Living in rural Iowa, I also had no experience with panhandlers and a homeless population. Farm life meant daily hard work and that's what I grew up with. Walking to work one day not long after I started, a homeless man approached me and asked for money. I won't pull any punches here about my response: "Get a @##$%-ing job."

And then went on to engage in an argument with him about panhandling and could not fathom why he didn't have a job and was more shocked that he just flat out asked for money.

A co-worker, Devon White (and I hope Devon finds me again as a result of writing this book), probably saved my life without me realizing it at the time. He grabbed my arm and pulled me away from my argument asking me what I thought I was doing. "Devon, he came up to me and asked for money!" Devon told me that I could end up hurt or dead. He then proceeded to tell me to never make eye contact with anyone. I said, "You're telling this girl from Iowa to never make eye contact?" This did *not* make sense to me. However, from then on, he walked me home from work every night and waited outside my hotel in the mornings to walk me to work. Clearly, he knew I'd talk with everyone.

At the time, I didn't understand his need to help me, but looking back, I recognize that I completely lacked "street smarts." I was only farm smart. It was a hard lesson but contributed to who I am today.

This was a case of being extremely too fearless because I didn't know what I didn't know. Based on my experiences in Iowa, we picked people up off the street and gave them rides; they never asked for money! Devon coached me on street smarts and taught me never to make eye contact with anyone. Okay, for the short stint I remained in the northeast for two and a half years, I did what he told me, but I'm still from Iowa and we make eye contact.

Consider This...

Darren Hardy, a success mentor, has said:

The activities you are most afraid of are the activities that can cause a breakthrough in your success. Step into them.

Let's dissect this. When there's an activity that I'm afraid of, I feel jittery and that I'm going out on a ledge, completely unsure if this is the right thing to do. I assure you, I had plenty of jitters when I considered my move to Philadelphia!

In all fairness and what I've learned is that when you're feeling that way, there's something exciting on the other side. In order to get there and reap the benefits, you simply have to do it.

You can put reason around it and think about it, but those jitters mean you are making yourself vulnerable and stepping outside of your comfort zone. When we're vulnerable is when we learn the most and when we grow the most. Too many people envision success at one end of the spectrum and failure at the other, like opposite ends of a line. That is the wrong image. Both failure and success work in tandem, and failure isn't the opposite of success, it's part of success. As Thomas Edison said, "I have not failed. I've just found 10,000 ways that won't work."

While you should never let success go to your head, you should never let failure get to your heart.

I assure you: There is zero possibility for growth inside of your own comfort zone. Break out!

Fearless

Chapter Three:

Failure IS an Option

In the movie *Apollo 13*, one of the classic lines to come out of it was: "Failure is not an option." Okay, in the case of NASA needing to get three astronauts back to earth from a failed moon landing, I'll agree that failure wasn't an option. However....

In the case of ordinary experiences, not only is failure an option, it's practically a requirement. You see, failure is first and foremost a teacher.

Most adults will tell you they "learned" how to ride a bicycle, but let's dive into that word and concept: learn. Learning to ride a bicycle (or anything) is really about all the failures that occurred before successfully balancing, pedaling, and steering. Those failures all contributed to you gaining enough confidence to ride the bicycle. I'm sure it was trial and error, getting on, losing balance and putting feet on the ground, or steering into something and crashing. Getting back on and trying again. You learned by failing.

Some people might call it "learning," but I prefer to think that failure was your necessary, if sometimes, painful teacher. I already shared that I was riding a motorcycle by the age of nine. Well, when I was 14, my father said, "Shell go get in the grain truck." Now the grain truck was a vehicle that carried 300 bushels of corn with a bushel weighing about 60 pounds or about nine tons. It's a big truck... with a manual transmission. Despite never having driven any vehicle, my dad directed me into the truck and told me to start it.

I turned the key and nothing happened. Next instructions: "Put your foot on the clutch and press down." Now when I turned the key, it turned over. Great. Now what? In his simple instructions I should put it in gear, release the clutch, and "just start driving." Now, if you've ever learned to drive a stick-shift, you know that there is an art to releasing the clutch or the truck will buck and stall. Of course, I popped the clutch, and I'll assure you, a nine-ton truck bucks pretty hard before it stalls.

"Do it again and learn to feel where the clutch pulls and engages." A review of the position of first gear, depressed clutch, turned key, and slowly released the clutch, and we went for a ride down the road with me at the wheel. End of formal lesson with the next instructions to meet him at the cornfield that afternoon… and he'd load it with corn for *me* to drive it to the elevator. What?!?

The point of the story is that I learned by failing. I can't say my dad was a good teacher, but failure certainly was, and that is probably what he already knew and figured failure would always be a better teacher anyway. The best lesson through all of the failures was that they weren't fatal and I always came out on the other side with more experience and more knowledge… knowledge fully imprinted on my brain.

Fast forward to the point in my career when I am working in real estate. I'd taken an online course and was working with a Realtor® flipping houses. The time came for me to "fire" him.

"Jim, I want to do this on my own now. You've inspired me to go it alone. I don't want your help anymore."

"Oh, Mechiel, you can't. You need my help. You'll learn the hard way. You'll *fail*."

I stuck to my decision, knowing that I would make mistakes and actually wanted to make those mistakes. I knew it would be the best way to learn. He reluctantly supported me, and we're still friends to this day.

Off I went to create my own world. I found and bought a house, and Jim allowed me to also use his construction crew and offered pointers as I went. I gutted and refinished the house in four months, and I'll tell you: It was beautiful… and then I tried to sell it. After a week on the market, there was no interest, no movement, no nothin'. As it turned out, there'd been a murder just a few houses away, and the guy had buried his wife in the backyard. Yeah, that'll quickly make a neighborhood pretty undesirable for a home purchase. Not to be deterred, I turned it into a rental instead. Yes, it was a flip that turned into a flop that could have been worse if not for "plan B" to rent it out. To this day, that particular house is not in my inventory, as my tenants have purchased it from me, another investor strategy.

To Jim's defense, he was right – I made mistakes! I learned that I paid too much for the house; I put too much money into it; and then it didn't sell.

If you want to call it *learning*, feel free to call it learning. For me, I embrace it as failure. The more times you fail, the better you're going to get. Don't be afraid to fail. It *is* an option.

Take a moment right now to look back on your own failures and determine how failure was your teacher to allow you to get to the desired result. What lessons did failure teach that you easily recall to this day?

Perfectionism

There is an exorbitant amount of time and energy wasted in the pursuit of perfection, and it's no wonder. The sense of perfection is pretty much the foundation of the education system. This became quite apparent to me in college. Having grown up on the farm and learning by failing, now I faced professors who all had the same agenda: perfection in the form of getting A's and B's. Grades below that indicated that you were a failure.

Failure was taking on the opposite context of what I knew it to be my whole life. Failure was seen as a stigma rather than an important teacher. It made no sense to me. I wanted the space and time to try and then fail, but the system was forcing perfection on me… or trying to. Perfection and good grades would lead to a better job. But would I really be any smarter not having the benefit of failure and its accompanying lessons?

Taking my own approach, I earned my degree in under three years and landed my first J.O.B. (Just Over Broke) In that J.O.B., I experienced much of the same – a demand to be perfect without making mistakes. Every J.O.B. I've ever had, except for one, expected perfection. If you weren't perfect, you'd be "written up." According to the rules, a certain number of "write ups" led to being fired. Personally, it was counterproductive to everything I'd ever learned growing up.

Most employers and managers use the carrot approach – an incentive, and that incentive is typically money. Perform this way without mistakes and get more money.

Employers have not liked me much because I've never been motivated by money. My motivation has always been recognition for a job well done and the space to be creative. I believe that sort of environment – one that demands perfection – and its companion incentive isn't healthy, nor does it allow for creative experimentation. Fear of failure stifles innovation.

It took a while to realize I was in the wrong environment. I needed to be my own boss, and as I look at where I am today, I realize I've come full circle to reflect where my father and grandfather were. As farmers, they were effectively in the real estate business, and now so am I.

Failing Toward Success

While failure is generally not fatal, you do have to get back up after failing, persevere, brush yourself off, apply the lesson, and move on. Consider some of these incredibly successful people who've failed their way toward success.

> *"Failure is simply the opportunity to begin again, this time more intelligently."*
>
> **~ Henry Ford**

J.K. Rowling, author of the *Harry Potter* series, shared these words during a Harvard commencement speech: "I had failed on an epic scale. An exceptionally short-lived marriage had imploded, and I was jobless, a lone parent, and as poor as it is possible to be in modern Britain, without being homeless. The fears that my parents had had for me, and that I had had for myself, had both come to pass, and by every usual standard, I was the biggest failure I knew." She believed in herself and her work and persevered. Depending on who's doing the reporting, her worth now ranges from $650 million to $1.2 billion.

I'll share another example that is not at all meant to be political but simply the story of someone who failed... but then went on the highest office in the land: Donald J. Trump. He had 13 failed businesses before he ran against a very competitive and experienced field to win the Republican nomination for president in 2016 and then went on to win the White House. "Sometimes by losing a battle, you need to find a new way to win the war." ~ Donald Trump.

Albert Einstein, whose name is now synonymous with genius and intelligence, was denied entrance to Zurich Polytechnic School. He persevered and went on to win the Nobel prize in physics, and his research has had an extraordinary impact on the world. In his estimation, "Success is failure in progress."

"I've missed more than 9,000 shots in my career. I've lost almost 300 games. Twenty-six times, I've been trusted to make the game-winning shot and missed. I've failed over and over and over again in my life. And that is why I succeed." Michael Jordan explains exactly what I'm talking about.

Very simply, if you aren't willing to fail, you will never really succeed.

Consider This...

Rich Dad Poor Dad author, Robert Kiyosaki:

Create an environment for people to fail, to learn, and to grow. Your team will be stronger and so will your success.

The most innovative companies and the best managers know the importance of creating an environment in which failure is not only acceptable, it is encouraged.

Now, it's important to keep in mind that the key regarding failing toward success is to learn… to apply the lesson. Go ahead and make mistake after mistake after mistake. Your goal isn't to avoid mistakes; you goal is not to make the same mistake twice. When that happens, then yes, failure will prevent you from moving forward.

When failure occurs and mistakes happen, don't blindly rush ahead. Stop and take time to evaluate what went wrong, why it went wrong, and what you can do the next time around to avoid *that* from happening again. Your next attempt may fail again but fail differently. Ditto to the subsequent attempt. Just remember: figure out what went wrong and why, then try something different.

Failure IS an Option

Chapter Four:

From Planting to Harvest

By now, you know I grew up on a farm and in a multi-generation farming family. Perhaps you can relate or perhaps farming is a complete unknown to you with food production for you beginning at the grocery store. Regardless, you know that it begins with planting seeds, but farming is so much more involved than that.

In fact, there are actually different methods of planting seeds. First and foremost, farming is heavily impacted by weather, and most farmers are also very good meteorologists, able to predict the weather by the smell of the air. You can feel the change in barometric pressure easily, and you can read the sky. You also become adept at translating exactly what the wind is telling you.

In most agrarian situations, and for me in Iowa, there are four seasons: spring, summer, fall, and winter. Spring is a time of renewal, and the soil is prepared and seeds are planted. Our crops consisted of corn, soybeans, and hay for the cows. Seed planting could occur in a row, one at a time, or they could be broadcast, spreading multiple seeds at once.

When the spring months turned to summer, it was a time of prosperous growth... and weed control. Once crops began to grow, herbicides were applied to maintain a healthy soil and allow the desired crops to pull nutrients out of it rather than letting the weeds steal those precious ingredients from the soil. Weeds are notorious for robbing nitrogen, needed for the healthy green of any plant – the chlorophyll that is essential for photosynthesis, allowing plants to convert light to energy.

Fall, of course, is the time for harvest. All the field crops are cut and placed in drying bins, apples are gathered, and all garden vegetables are canned or frozen.

Now you may think that these three seasons are the most important; however, it's actually in winter when you actually capitalize and truly reap the benefit of the efforts of the rest of the year. On a large scale, crops are hauled and sold to elevators, and on a smaller scale, farm families enjoy the garden vegetables that have been preserved through the winter months. Winter is also a time of important preparation for the next growing season. Equipment is cleaned, repaired as needed, often repainted. Taxes are paid. Seed supplies are acquired for the next season. The winter is also a time of rejuvenation both giving the soil and those who work it time to rest.

In real estate, I use the same philosophy; however, it doesn't correlate to the actual "seasons" so to speak. I plant seeds by networking and looking for properties to buy. When I find property, now I do my due diligence to see if the property meets my criteria. I evaluate it to validate its cash flow. After the evaluation, I'll make an offer. If the offer is accepted, I'll purchase the property. Depending on the exit strategy, I'll create a plan and put that plan in motion. In the situation of my first commercial real estate venture with an apartment complex, I held that property for one year, improved the property, and sold it for huge profits. Analogous to farming, it went from planting to harvest.

Regular Routines

The pattern of spring, summer, fall, winter routine continued for me for the first 18 years of my life. My life was centered around routines and task-driven activities. It was the ultimate in terms of a "wash, rinse, repeat" routine and cycle and was embedded deep inside my brain. It also provided a foundation of developing a significant amount of discipline, consistency, determination, reward for hard work, persistence, respect, and accountability.

Now, if you are currently employed and working for someone else, your routine probably looks something like this: Get up at 5:00; hit the gym; be at work by 8:00; home by 6:00; eat dinner; relax (read, watch TV, etc.); in bed by 10:00. Repeat for five days and then engage in your weekend routine: Sleep in on Saturday, mow the grass, clean the pool, run errands, laundry, and perhaps treat yourself to dining out. Sunday may include church and something a bit more relaxing… to get ready for a repeat of this seven-day cycle.

As an entrepreneur and working for myself, I have more control over my time. My schedule is: wake at 6:00; reflect, read, and exercise; attack my previously set agenda for the day; meet with clients to discuss transactions; set weekly time to meet with my mentor and set aside time to write a book; weave in time for continuous networking on a daily basis; and I focus on my swim lane.

> *Developing a routine is not the same as maintaining the status quo. The former will make you more productive; the latter likely keeps you stuck in a rut.*

The importance of routine, even a varied one like mine, is that it keeps you focused and streamlines your processes. In the IT world, I followed a pre-established project plan for task completion, but I also structured my daily and weekly activities both inside the framework of my job and for personal goals and activities. Mondays were meetings with customers and status meetings. Tuesdays were team meetings and task discussion and planning. Wednesdays were time to update projects and write status reports. Thursdays were meetings with executives to provide updates, and Fridays were left open.

Here are five important routines that you should consider:

1. Wake up at your perfect time, and wake up at the same time every day, even on weekends, to keep your personal rhythms running smoothly. You'll find you no longer need an alarm clock; I haven't used one for years.

2. Eliminate decision-making tasks first thing in the morning (emails, texts, phone calls, etc.). It's a very rare person who truly gets out of bed and hits the ground running at full speed and firing on all cylinders.

3. Create a morning routine that you'll use to focus your mind. Mine starts with a deep breath and time allotted to reading my devotional.

4. Start moving and hydrate. Your body actually dehydrates while you sleep. I drink an entire bottle of water before hitting the gym.

5. Get productive. Now that you've warmed up both your mind and body, you're ready to tackle

your daily agenda. Now you're ready to move at full speed. I also suggest you write your agenda the night before, so you don't waste time figuring out what you should begin with.

Waste Not....

Farm lessons were not easy lessons. I shared in the "Failure IS an Option" chapter about my father teaching me to drive the grain truck, and there's more to that story. When he had me drive the truck to the field, he was there combining corn. My job was to drive to where he was so that he could dump the first load into the truck, and I was to drive it to the elevator. It was a true lesson in the difference between high and low gears. Low gear was needed when hauling heavy loads – the difference between an empty and now a full grain truck. You had to be at the right speed to get into high gear. After a few trips, I got the hang of it, and my goal became: how quickly could I get into high gear and run at a cruising speed?

At the elevator, I became pretty popular. One, I was a girl, and two, I needed help unloading. The work became fun. The boys working there didn't know me. I was just this girl who showed up to the elevator to dump my corn. When they'd see me coming, they'd all be ready to help me. However, there wasn't much time to enjoy this aspect of the job. I had a schedule to maintain to return to the farm by the time my father was ready to dump the next load of harvested corn. The routine continued for several days until the field was completely harvested.

I thought I was pretty good at what I was doing; however, there was one major issue that quickly deflated my ego. One day during the harvest, my dad approached with his unmistakable, sideways pissed-off look. "Shell, you're driving way too fast. You need to slow down." He didn't say more than that. I couldn't figure out how he knew this? Did someone rat me out? My dad wasn't Paul Harvey and he wasn't going to "tell me the rest of the story." I wondered if he was timing my trips, but it was important for my trip to and from the elevator to coincide with his harvesting with the combine, so he wasn't wasting time waiting for me. If I didn't get back in time, he couldn't unload.

It took a few loads for me to figure out his mysterious puzzle. As I drove away with a load, I looked into the passenger side mirror and noticed that as the wind hit the corn in my truck, it was blowing it out and onto the side of the road. Suddenly, I was focused on and painfully aware of all the corn along the side of the road. It was corn for which my father wouldn't be paid. It was wasted. The light bulb went on, and from that point forward, I drove much more responsibly. It was slower on the way to the elevator and faster on the way back.

Sometimes getting to the finish line doesn't mean how fast you get there. In IT, we measured our projects by Scope, Time, and Budget. Our customers got to pick two; you can't have a successful project trying to make sure you're in scope, on budget, and on time. The priority must be set at the beginning of the project to ensure success.

Seasonal Lessons

Spring on the farm consisted of "walking beans" that meant walking up and down the rows, cutting out weeds with a bean hook. Sexy, right? Nope. It was blood, sweat, and… more sweat. Tears weren't allowed. Picking up rocks was another task. After every winter, the earth would reveal its rocks, and some were large enough (I thought they were boulders!) that they would damage equipment during planting. Dad's solution was for the kids and Mom to get the tractor and a wagon and gather them and unload them elsewhere on the property. It was our least favorite job, and we all complained, including Mom.

In summer, at age 9, it became my duty to take care of 150 cattle. It included doing a head count on the cows when they began calving. I had to tag each calf's ear and check the fences to ensure they were secure. Checking the fence meant 1.5 miles of walking, and if a cow got out, I had to herd them back. Dad's solution was to get me a dirt bike, so I could complete the task and report back much faster.

Fall was harvest. No rest for the weary. We fought with the weather to get all the crops out of the ground before it started snowing. It became a high adrenaline activity from sunup to sundown and sometimes working into the dark, just to get those crops out of the field and into the drying bins. Often, we'd help other farmers if they were behind.

Winter is revenue time for farmers; it's when they can cash in on three seasons of effort. It's also a time when loans are due. As a farmer, whatever loan you might have taken out was due as an annual payment. There were no monthly payments as you might have in a typical loan.

Sowing, Reaping, and Changing

Whether or not you knew a thing about farming before you picked up this book, I know you knew that everything grows from a seed. That is entirely true in your life and your business as well. As I always say, "In order for things to happen, you have to make them happen." If you're sitting around doing nothing all day, then nothing is going to happen, and you are going to yield nothing. If you are stuck in a rut – whether it's in your career, your relationship, etc. – unless you do something, you will remain in that very rut. You will not accomplish any goals and you will achieve nothing except probably frustration and negativity, which are two incredibly dangerous mindsets.

In order for anything to happen, it must start with you. You've probably heard that what you sow is exactly what you reap. Whether you broadcast seeds by scattering them widely or plant them in a nice neat row, you absolutely have to be planting seeds or you will harvest nothing; you will achieve nothing. Admittedly, not every seed grows either literally or in this analogy, so it's important to cast more seeds than you think you need.

Variety and change are also important. While we grew corn and soybeans for sale, our garden had a wide assortment of vegetables. After all, who wants to eat the same thing all the time? It wasn't all tomatoes; it wasn't all beans; it wasn't all peppers. Variety is important in your diet, and it is important in your life as well. And that brings us to change.

For some people, change is actually a four-letter word. Most people are creatures of habit. You may be guilty of that as well, and habit can be fine… to a point. Yes, doing some things habitually can save time and keep you focused as we covered earlier in this chapter. But when it comes to really achieving big things, you gotta shake things up! Too many people get stuck getting up at the same time, doing the exact same thing, going to the same nine-to-five job, returning home, making dinner, going to bed... and repeat... and repeat... and repeat. There is little room for achievement in that formula!

Even on the farm, despite its consistency, there were times to shake things up. Planting the same crop in the same field year after year led to soil nutrient depletion, leading to less than desirable results. The same thing easily happens in your life as well.

Embracing change is huge. Once you adapt to embracing rather than repelling change, the opportunities open up before you, and they are endless. New opportunities lead to growth. Growth leads to achievement. Achievement leads to success.

But let's face it. We are hardwired to resist change. Our brains like the predictable, and they like to be in control. Predictable control is where your brain feels safest. As far as your brain is concerned, moving outside of your comfort zone could be dangerous... even deadly. That said, while your brain gravitates toward the status quo, your brain is also flexible and can be molded into something different.

> *A bend in the road isn't the end of the road... unless you fail to make the turn.*

Start by accepting uncertainty. You can't control everything and there will always be uncertainties. And while you can't control a particular situation, you can control how you perceive it. Instead of focusing on worry, focus on the amazing outcomes that can result.

Consider the best and worst case scenarios. More often than not, the worst case isn't usually that bad, so once you determine it, let it go. For example, you decide to jump into entrepreneurship and leave your paycheck-driven job behind. The worst case scenario is that you may end up getting another job... if things don't work out. However, I want you to focus on all the fantastic results that can come from being your own boss. Keep the possibilities and not the problems in your head.

Decide to take a risk. Risk enhances your life. If you stick to what your brain wants – predictable control – you're missing out on all the possibilities and opportunities for incredible outcomes. You are missing out on growth. Don't fixate on failure. Sure, things may not go exactly as planned, but that does not equate to failure. If you're struggling with this, go back and reread "Failure IS an Option."

Start with small steps. Conquer little fears first because conquering fear is a learned skill. Think about all of the skills you've mastered in your life. Conquering fear is simply something else to learn.

Make sure your excitement about winning is always greater than your fear of losing. Look back only long enough to draw and apply the lesson of your mistakes. Then immediately look forward and visualize how you are going to use that lesson to leap forward in your progress.

Consider This...

Elon Musk, business magnate and visionary has said:

If you want to grow a giant redwood, you need to make sure the seeds are okay, nurture the sapling, and work out what might potentially stop it from growing all the way along. Anything that breaks it at any point stops that growth.

Coast redwood trees are the tallest trees in the world. They not only seem to grow to reach for the stars, they also serve as host to sky-high ecosystems in their canopies, and their roots actually intertwine with other surrounding redwoods to support each other and increase their stability. And they have really thick skin with bark that is up to a foot thick to help them survive forest fires and fend off damaging insects.

Envision your business as a redwood tree. Select the right seed and nurture it. Consider everything that might break your business in its early stages and plan to mitigate all of those hazards. Develop a network for support, and become resilient to criticism. Encourage growth (of your business and yourself) and you will begin reaching for the stars as well.

From Planting to Harvest

Chapter Five:

Don't Care What Others Think

In addition to growing up on a farm, the community around us was very small... and everyone chit chatted. It seemed everyone knew everyone else's business. Having said that, do you think that my grandfather would have invented the round hay baler if he let anyone else – or what they had to say – influence him? Of course, the answer is a great big "no"!

My grandfather had a great attitude, and it rubbed off on me, and it is certainly one worth emulating. He didn't care what other people thought of him. Instead, he was purpose driven to invent and produce. Once he began working on the baler, he stayed focus on the end result, and that end result was something that would yield dividends on the farm. Grandpa didn't care what anyone else had to say about him and his efforts. Instead of wasting any time caring or worrying about what others thought, he simply went and did it.

If you want to be successful and achieve your goals, you must adopt my Grandpa's attitude. If you stop to consider what everyone else has to say and let others around you influence your actions, you will never get where you want to go. Instead, stay focused. Don't worry (or stop worrying if that's something you do now!) about what others think and be the exception. It's the way you can stand out in the crowd and get noticed.

Make other people wonder about what you're working on. It's a great way to drum up curiosity, and by doing so, you might just attract the very person you need in your life at that moment.

Overcoming Financial Worries

In my project management days, I joined a team with a much larger geographic footprint and greater variety of product offerings than my previous employer. It was a step up the career ladder for me and would expand my depth of knowledge and challenge me to learn new things. Instead of solely implementing back office accounting solutions, I would gain knowledge about front-end software, including CRM systems, data conversions, and heavy integration between front and back office workings.

It didn't take long for my new employer to believe in me as I moved from small gigs and assignments to working with the more difficult client personalities, ultimately landing on working on a $3 million-dollar deal. That particular client chose all of the core modules in the product plus HR and payroll. The project included five outside vendors and a number of required integrations; the data migration alone would have been its own very large project. This three-year engagement was by far the most complicated to coordinate and difficult to maneuver, but it was incredibly rewarding to see it through to fruition and success.

However, by the end of that three-year stint, events unfolded that actually set me back another three years. In 2007, I lost my dad very unexpectedly. He was my rock, and losing him felt like my foundation had crumbled. The relationship I was in would be tested... and failed. The very work I loved doing felt like a chore, and I was stressed out to the point of depression. Any and all medications my doctor suggested simply made it worse. My company chose to part ways with me, and a day after that I learned that my best friend had died from colon cancer. Then came my own diagnosis of being in the early stages of menopause.

It was three years of my life in which I didn't really sleep and don't recall actually accomplishing anything. BUT... did I stop moving forward? No. Did I move at a slower pace? Yes. Did I take time for myself? Absolutely.

The day my J.O.B. quit me was actually the most liberating day I've ever experienced. That occurrence along with learning that my best friend had passed illuminated my knowledge of what I needed to do: I needed to leave and go spend time with her family. I was a godparent without hesitation, so I flew to Tennessee and stayed for two weeks, helping her family in any way I could.

Did I worry about where the next paycheck might come from? The honest answer was no. I can't say for certain how I knew everything would be okay, but I knew that what I couldn't worry about was what others might think. Looking back, my dad never had a J.O.B. In fact, growing up, none of the adults in my life had a J.O.B., so why did I feel I needed to have one? Why was I depending on others for my income and well-being? I had more questions than answers.

While visiting my friend, Patsy in North Carolina, it finally hit me. I had reached a level of comfort and could sit in silence to hear what it was I was supposed to do. Had I just had a "bucket time" experience or was it something even grander? I was at peace with my decision and, again, chose not to worry what anyone else might think about it.

When I got home, I put my plan into action, making several calls to my U.S.-based network and discovered I could subcontract my project management skills to other consultants and other Microsoft partners around the world. I had enough contacts that this would work, and my first company, Project Strategixx LLC, was born in 2009. I was embarking on a new journey; however, there was one major issue that would set me back. With no income for six months, I had just finished the construction work on my primary residence. The bottom fell out of the market, leaving me with property that was worth less than when I started.

For six months, I worked on a project-by-project basis, marketing my skills, until I could modify my mortgage. This became my full focus, and I produced several inches' worth of documents to satisfy the need. I felt like the lender was piling on requirements because they wanted me to fail. However, not caring what others thought, I was determined not to lose my house. They would schedule calls and on-site meetings, and I was always fully prepared. I could see the light at the end of the tunnel and knew there was no way I'd be declined, but I had to attend one last meeting – the budget meeting to prove I knew how to budget.

> *Worry is a waste of your precious time and energy. You can't change the past, so focus on what you want in the future, and put a plan in place today to achieve it.*

I thought, "I handled a $3 million-dollar budget for a project in which the money wasn't even mine. This will be a slam dunk."

Before leaving for the meeting, I sent my budget to the Director of Modifications, hoping to save us both time in the meeting. I arrived early, and the director called me back. He said, "I kid you not, Mechiel. I don't know why we put you through this lengthy process. After reviewing your budget, you do not need to be here."

"Wonderful," I replied. "Just sign this line right here and I'll be on my way." I had everything I needed and had just saved my home. Had I worried about what others thought of my approach, I would have wasted time and energy that was clearly better spent on what I was determined to do.

Now I was free to travel for assignments and did so for the next three years, across the U.S. and in Bermuda, working on some amazing projects and meeting some amazing people. Living as an entrepreneur actually felt like home to me. There was a shift in my thinking and I began leaning more toward real estate (now owning six rental properties and a vacation cabin in Tennessee) with less focus on IT and project management as a source of income. Some probably thought that, having survived what I'd gone through, I should stay the course and continue doing what I'd been doing. I didn't care what they thought. I started taking IT projects on a part-time basis to give me more time to focus on developing real estate income.

A former client asked to hire me on a part-time basis for six months to help them clear a specific challenge. Of course, I wanted to help them... three days a week to allow my real estate company to gain traction. Three years later, unemployment was knocking on the door, but this time I was ready for it and encouraged my employer to let me go. It caught them off guard, and I didn't care what they thought. There was new management brought in, and I could see the writing on the wall. "Your job has been eliminated." My reply: "Great. When's my last day?" Thirty days later, I was gone and never looked back.

Get Uncomfortable

Some might say I'm lucky. But I'll tell you this: There is no luck in anything. It is always hard work that pays off for you, coupled with your determination, to get what you want and achieve your goals.

Hand in hand with not caring what others think is embracing the uncomfortable. Being uncomfortable empowers you. As soon as that last J.O.B., ended, I signed up for Robert Kiyosaki (author of *Rich Dad, Poor Dad*) six-month training that cost $6,000. I learned how to evaluate properties, but most importantly I learned to change my mindset.

To this point, I'd been taught and embraced the idea that working to get good grades and striving for perfection was the key to success. Well, now at age 53, I wasn't feeling perfect, fulfilled, successful… or happy. The problem was my mindset.

To put some perspective on this lesson, let me go back almost 20 years. Something monumental occurred that I wouldn't recognize until much later. My girlfriend wanted to relocate to North Carolina, and I provided some solutions by buying both her townhouse as an investment rental property and… Buccaneer football tickets. Both purchases would go on to fuel my own fire.

I had no idea how to first find tenants and then, even more importantly, qualify them. Rental laws were unfamiliar to me as were tracking rental expenses and income. I was at a real disadvantage with seasoned tenants, and the best I could offer was my charming and helpful personality. Tenants became friends, and I thought if I was engaging, attentive, and friendly, that would be enough to avoid being screwed. However, there were hard lessons on creative financing based on a tenant's inability to pay, and I also quickly learned about evictions. That experience led me to learn how to avoid the eviction process in the first place!

With those lessons in place, I purchased another townhouse and enjoyed the role of landlord and real estate investor so much that I purchased six more plus a vacation cabin. My new game was buying a foreclosure, placing a tenant, and then buy-and-hold. I also dabbled in a short-term rental property using a property management company. When I felt they were taking too much of the pie, I fired them and listed with VRBO. There was quite a lot of work that went into this approach – photos, hiring cleaning and maintenance companies, responding to inquiries. I found myself attached to my phone 24/7 as the app rates your property based on your own reaction time... at a time I was still working in my full-time IT job. This real estate venture did not align with my lifestyle, and when the time to sell was right, I got out of vacation rentals.

My hunger for real estate did not manifest until 2009, but I didn't really make it happen until 2017 at age 53. Looking back, in '09, I should have moved with the speed and passion that I applied in '17, thinking what those results might have been. I don't dwell on or regret the delay, but I want you to use my own experience as a guide. If you have a fleeting thought and a passion that keeps tugging at you, either consciously or somewhat subconsciously, take action now and make it happen!

It's Okay to Say No

As I mentioned in the chapter about failure, I'd been working with a mentor and decided it was time to part ways and for me to strike out on my own. He tried to dissuade me, but I knew I had to do this and could not worry about what he thought.

I purchased a property based on what I'd learned in my training. However...

1. I didn't purchase at the right price.
2. I put too much money into it.
3. The project took too much time.
4. The house wouldn't sell.

It was beautiful and fully renovated, but a news story hit about a man killing his wife and burying her in the back yard... just six blocks away. Neighborhood prices fell $10k in a week. On the bright side, I knew from my project management work that I simply had to move onto Plan B, which was to find good tenants. The tenants I found have actually bought the property from me. But wait, there's more.

While managing this project, I stumbled into another deal for a commercial property. Another Realtor brought this listing to my attention. Since 2005, it had been my goal to own commercial property, and here was an eight-unit apartment complex on the water for $595,000. After a week of discussion, I decided to see it. During the walk through, the listing agent fully disclosed that the AC units were 28 years old and there was a sea wall erosion issue, but he already had a repair bid of $20,000. Using my handy dandy evaluation spreadsheet, I determined the asking price was way off base. I declined to offer.

A month later, the price dropped to $495,000. I passed again as the numbers did not align for me. A few weeks later, it dropped again. Now my interest was piqued. I offered $484,500, and they accepted. The inspection confirmed what had been disclosed, but all the repairs and replacements would need to happen sooner than later. I renegotiated the offer down another $50,000, and the sellers accepted. I remember thinking, "This process was way too easy."

The first big hurdle of which I was unaware was to find a lender, being cautioned that residential and commercial projects were far different. I needed to find a lender to write a commitment letter within the next five... hours! Applying for a loan is a daunting task – almost requiring providing blood type and first born. I followed the advice to take to the internet and actually found a lender who believed in me and provided that letter three hours later!

Now I had 30 days to seal the deal with the lender, but they ultimately declined, and it was back to the drawing board. My drive to succeed was misplaced. I made all the wrong moves and was definitely living up to my desire to learn by making mistakes – epic mistakes! But I didn't care what others thought. I was pursuing a goal and maintained a laser focus.

Not unlike my first residential property purchase with a neighborhood murder tanking prices, I learned the area around my commercial property was becoming depressed, without a lot of job opportunities, other than those in the service industry, making it difficult to raise rents to where they needed to be. The previous owners had also under-represented the cost of utilities – expenses that cut well into my profits. Passing them along to tenants wasn't a real option.

Yes, I made plenty of mistakes as I pursued this goal, and it ultimately had a very profitable ending, I'm happy to say (as I'll share later). The real point and the big lesson is that if you put stock in others' opinions about your dreams and goals, you'll probably never reach them. So you have a choice: care about what others think or go for it and achieve what you set out to do. Don't care and dream big!

Consider This...

Chinese philosopher, Lao Tzu said:

Care about what other people think and you will always be their prisoner.

So, do you want to be true to yourself or do you want to place yourself in a self-imposed jail created by the opinions of others?

Stay focused on what it is you want to achieve and disregard everything else. Now, I'm not suggesting that you trample on other people or ignore the needs of those you care about. But I do want you to put far less stock in their opinions about your goals. The only exception to that is to consider the opinions of those who have already achieved what you want to do. Notice I said "consider" their opinions. There's a big difference between consideration and implementation.

Chapter Six:

Embrace Risk

Growing up in my family, there was no real fear of risk. Instead, there was a "can do" attitude about nearly everything. No one ever cautioned me, "Before you get on that bicycle, you'd better watch out for that tree." It was up to me to figure that out or hit the tree and learn the hard way. While riding my motorcycle during a storm, the wind was blowing hard and the grass was so tall that I didn't see the tree stump. Yup, I hit it, and I went one way and the bike went another. I rode as fast as I could back to the house. Even if storms threatened, I wasn't cautioned about waiting to trek over a mile to check the cows. It was up to me to learn that heading out in a storm was a stupid and dangerous idea.

Risk in my family was backed up by believing in someone. For me, it was believing in my dad. When we were in his plane and he shut the engine off, my heart sank right into my stomach; however, I believed in him and knew he would never do anything to hurt us. Of course, he'd restart the engine. Risk wasn't on the radar. Things happened, we dealt with it, and all lived another day.

I'm not suggesting your ignore risk, rather evaluate it. Risk assessment became part of every project plan when I was working in IT. I had to take classes on how to properly evaluate risk; it did add a whole new layer to my project management bag of tricks. Before any project plan was implemented, we did a risk analysis to determine and define all the risks as well as the probabilities that those risks might actually occur. We then implemented a detailed plan to mitigate risk.

At the time, my boss, Curtis, would say, "Nobody dies." Good news, to be sure. He knew he might be throwing us to the wolves but also knew we'd learn, persevere, and come out stronger and smarter in the end. This lesson was all too familiar to me. It was the same one I'd grown up with on the farm.

Risk has actually been comfortable for me. As a benefit, embracing risk developed my ability to solve issues and overcome challenges. When you understand the risks and what you need to do to mitigate them, you can move forward more easily. Piece of cake, so to speak. My ability to move past the risks brought the vision into focus.

For example, when I purchased that eight-unit apartment complex, I was so focused on the vision of what this property could become that even when I blatantly saw the risks with the purchase, the outcome of what it could and did become far outweighed the issues. Issues can always be solved. Knowing the story, you know that I evaluated the risks but still moved forward.

> *"If you are not willing to risk the unusual, you will have to settle for the ordinary."*
>
> *~ Jim Rohn*

One of the big things I learned from that experience is the benefit of surrounding yourself with people who have greater experience and knowledge. That's how I ultimately was able to join forces with the right team in order to sell the commercial property before the expenses became too great and the one-year balloon payment was due.

Most people fail because they are unwilling to take the risk in the first place. If you find yourself in this category, I implore you to start changing your mindset; otherwise, you will never grow. If you're okay with your own status quo, then it's fine to continue avoiding risk. If you want to achieve more, then you must begin to embrace risk.

I'm not suggesting you be reckless. There's a big difference between risk and recklessness. The former involves learning about what can go wrong and having a plan in place to mitigate those things and deal with them if they occur. Keep in mind that there is a direct correlation between risk and reward. Consider financial investing as an example. Those who aren't willing to risk likely put their money in a plain ol' savings account or CD and get very little in the way of a return on their investment. Those who take some risk (e.g., investing in stocks or real estate) stand to enjoy great returns. Simply look at Wall Street's performance over time. The returns are always greater when there is some risk involved.

Yes, you can "lose it all"; however, if you first do your homework in assessing the risk of any investment, you're taking steps to mitigate that risk. You might ask, "What if I fall?" And to that, I'll reply, "What if you fly?" Take the risk or lose the chance. Honestly, life is all about taking risks. If you risk nothing, you'll never learn what you're capable of.

Personally, I'm comfortable being a mover and shaker because that's where all the action is. Embracing risk is a must if you want to achieve your financial freedom.

Consider This...

Motivational speaker, Zig Ziglar said:

One of the main reasons people fail to reach their full potential is because they are unwilling to risk anything.

If you don't care about achieving your full potential and being successful, don't take a risk. Stay right where you are. If ordinary is okay for you, you can stop reading.

However, even if you find yourself on the path toward your goals and the success you want, there is still a need to take risks to further your achievement. We may never know when we've actually reached our full potential. Even if we're great... why can't we be just a little bit better. Take another risk and achieve even more.

Chapter Seven:

Discipline and Adaptability

Discipline, in my estimation, is not a noun. It's an action verb. Before I even learned the dictionary definition of discipline, I understood it inherently as a result of my upbringing and surroundings. The cows needed to be fed every day, twice a day – the first feeding at 5:00 a.m. before I went to school and then again when I got home from basketball practice. There were no other choices. You knew what was expected of you… and you just did it, no questions asked. Nor did you ask for help.

Days working in the field with Dad were hard days. We'd only stop for dinner, which is actually lunch to almost everyone else in the world. Mom prepared the meal, and we had about five minutes to eat. Then it was back to the field and back to work. No one-hour lunch break. That meant burning daylight, and to any farmer, daylight is a critical component of success. To this day, I'm still an early riser, and when my feet hit the floor, I'm "off to the races" for the day. I set an agenda and it's prioritized.

I was often thrown into situations in which I was left to figure out things on my own. Not all my decisions were sound; however, those that weren't were learning opportunities that forced me to adjust and move forward again. You may think that's a harsh way to grow up, but as a farmer's daughter, you cannot place me into a situation today in which I will be unable to find some solution. And solutions have gotten better and better as I've faced increasing numbers of decisions.

Discipline and adaptability were tested when I left for college. At 18, as I described earlier, I traveled five hours with my belongings in a horse trailer, was dropped off, and left alone. In that moment, I might have felt a bit of terror... or at least angst, but as I look back, I'm impressed with the way I handled the whole thing. Morning number one, I got up and got to class, and repeated that for the next 2.8 years without relying on anyone else. I knew my schedule, where I had to be and when, and exactly what I had to do.

It was a big change – life on the farm to life in a big city – and required me to adapt... and adapt quickly. I often wondered which was the easiest transition to which to adapt: me going from farm to city or city kids living on a farm. There was no shortage of changes: traffic, crowds, greater diversity and cultural exposures, and different lifestyles. But it seemed none of it bothered me.

With my post-college career move to Philadelphia, living in Chinatown for months without a car, I was certainly challenged to be adaptable. While I always thought farm kids had it tougher than city kids, I was gaining a new perspective. Philadelphia was way, way different than Iowa and even Kansas City, but once again, I knew where I had to be and when and what I had to do.

Once I had a car, I relocated to the Jersey side and had to learn to use mass transit and cope with commuting: 20-minute car ride, five-minute walk, 20-minute train ride, 15-minute walk. I had to gain street smarts that I hadn't needed up to this point in my life. Again, looking back, I had to adapt to succeed, and I learned lessons that became quite valuable during my project management years.

Discipline and adaptability are critical factors in successfully managing IT projects. This was true not only in the J.O.B., but in my case getting there. As a consultant, I had to travel quite a lot, needing to find hotels, learn navigation in new cities, and the best places to eat. While all cities have certain things in common, there is enough about each one to make them unique. Traveling to and working in Dallas is a far different experience than doing so in Hollywood or Bermuda. Fitting in with the on-site staffs was almost always necessary, and I assure you, the culture in Dallas and Bermuda are about as far apart as possible. An inability to adapt led to being removed from the project.

No matter where you are in life or where you're going, especially in today's world, you need the ability to stand out in a crowd and differentiate yourself from others. You will get noticed if you have discipline and are able to adapt to any situation.

Consider This...

Charles Darwin, naturalist and biologist observed:

It is not the strongest of the species that survives, nor the most intelligent. It is the one that is most adaptable to change.

While you have to be disciplined to be a successful entrepreneur, that discipline must always be coupled with adaptability. Your business ventures, and in fact, every aspect of your life will always change. Change is inevitable. Or as you've probably heard, the only thing that stays the same is that everything changes.

I want you to be disciplined but never at the expense of simultaneously being adaptable. When you combine those two, you are on your way to becoming unstoppable in achieving your goals and exactly what you set out to do.

Chapter Eight:

Attitude

Attitude is all about the way you carry yourself, including a settled way of thinking and feeling... about someone, something, your surroundings. Let's face it: We all have attitudes. It's our choice to determine and choose our attitude about anything and everything.

My Grandpa had a very fierce attitude, and it was obvious and prevalent in every conversation you had with him. In a nutshell, his attitude was that he didn't give "two shits" about what anyone else thought about him. While we hear about the "haters" in this day and age, my Grandpa had them back in the '80s. He set a good example, letting it all roll off his shoulders and never once letting anyone affect him or his decisions.

If it weren't for this staunch, believe-in-yourself attitude, he never would have gotten the round hay baler patented. The hurdles he had to clear to get the patent were unbelievable. Additionally, he was not only the inventor, he was the top sales and marketing force that made it successful. Without the right attitude, coupled with his persistence, Hay & Forage Industries in Hesston, Kansas would not have awarded him the contract and paid the licensing fees for the baler. As I recall, in order for Hay & Forage Industries to even consider the patent in the first place, Grandpa had to hire patent attorneys. Additionally, because he couldn't draw the pieces, he had to tear it apart to enable the blueprint attorneys to illustrate each and every part and working piece.

Despite this, Grandpa's attitude didn't change, and he did what he had to do to continue to move forward. In the end, his persistence paid off. He received the patent for the round hay baler on Oct. 24, 1978. However, even with the success, his attitude didn't change. With the patent in hand, the haters all began talking and chiming in, sometimes making life in a small town unbearable. Imagine him walking into a café with the locals who'd then slide over to the edge of the booth, preventing him from taking a seat.

Grandpa's attitude? Shrug it off and keep doing what he loved: inventing other farm machinery. This attitude migrated down the generations of our family – first to my father and then to me.

The real lesson here that underscores what we've covered in "Don't Care What Others Think" is not to let other people drag you down. You've heard, "Misery loves company," so you can be certain that less driven and less successful people would like nothing better than to drag you down to their level. That's their attitude (and fear)… not yours. Don't buy in to their thinking.

When I set off to ride my motorcycle, I put on my "attitude." What is it? Attitude is the confidence you need to do something. Sometimes that attitude – that confidence – isn't there. If you sense that attitude isn't 100 percent, listen to your gut and act accordingly.

One day, I garbed up to ride, and after traveling a short distance, I realized I didn't have confidence that day. I listened to my body, shared with my friends that I felt "I wasn't supposed to ride today," and I returned home. I'll share with you that I was pretty nervous and nerved up inside, so I paid attention to the signals and respected that my attitude and confidence had, for whatever reason, taken that day off. It hasn't happened since, but I'm glad I listened to that internal voice.

Running IT projects also brought out my attitude. Over the years, I had perfected my skills and the confidence that went along with doing so. I continued to get stronger and better at managing clients and finding solutions for them.

With experience in your field, you'll build your attitude. Your attitude will drive your confidence. This creates the foundation in which you can thrive to try new things. Trying new things allows you to grow and expand your knowledge.

Attitude vs. Attitudinal

There's a distinction between having attitude and being attitudinal. The latter involves raising your voice and openly arguing. Teenagers seem to have perfected the art of being attitudinal, and being attitudinal may well stem from lacking confidence. Having attitude is about speaking and communicating effectively and engaging with confidence to solve problems.

Here are five attitudes every entrepreneur must develop in order to run a prosperous business:

1. Passion: Be passionate about your ideas and goals.
2. Bravery: Entrepreneurs, like everyone else, do feel fear. Bravery is about how you face and overcome fear, not the lack of it.

3. Flexibility: Be able to bend with the twists and turns you encounter because there will always be twists, turns, and hurdles.
4. Strong work ethic: Working long hours pays off, and remember: the harder you work, the luckier you get.
5. Integrity: Be honest and have strong moral principles.

Your attitude influences every action you take. The right attitude generates the best outcomes and results. It encompasses a great deal about your mindset as well. When opportunity knocks on your door, do you race to answer it or complain about the noise? Yes, millions of words have been written about the "glass half empty or full" perspective.

> *Attitudinal is being argumentative; having attitude means confidence. Choose the later, always.*

You might believe that the smartest people are the most successful; however, studies show that attitude is a much better indicator of success than IQ. The most successful entrepreneurs share a growth mindset – the understanding that abilities can be developed. Remember Grandpa only had a seventh grade eduction. We will all have moments of feeling helpless, and success stems from our reaction to that feeling. We can crumble and succumb or we can learn from it and move forward again. Those who embrace a growth mindset don't feel helpless for long... if at all. A well-developed growth mindset and a feeling of helplessness cannot really coexist.

In order to be successful, you must be willing to risk and to fail… and then to learn, bounce back, and move forward again.

Consider This…

Philosopher and psychologist, William James said:

It is our attitude at the beginning of a difficult task which, more than anything else, will affect its successful outcome.

Your attitude is truly the driver of every outcome in your life. What you believe about yourself is always what will come to pass… good or bad.

Attitude

Chapter Nine:

Drive & Determination

Let me warn you right now: This chapter is not for the faint of heart. You may not appreciate the story I am about to share. However, I can guarantee you'll understand why I am choosing to share it with you in terms of the concept of drive and determination.

I had asked Dad to teach me how to trap raccoons. He didn't "teach me" as much as he simply told me what to do. He took me to the farm store where we purchased lure to be applied to sticks and plants along the riverside. This would attract raccoons to the places where I'd positioned traps. Once lured, the raccoon would smell the sardines I'd buried in a can at the riverbank. Finding the can, the trap would release and snap on their foot.

On day one, I rose at 5:00 a.m. and got on my dirt bike to check the six traps I'd set. Upon reaching the first one, I saw that I'd caught one. My instructions from my dad were to club its head with a piece of wrought iron. I'd never done anything like this, and my futile attempts led to frustration. The raccoon didn't die, and I quit. I returned home and got ready for school without checking the other traps.

Before I go further, farmers trapped raccoons because: 1) they were overpopulated; 2) they were eating our sweet corn crops; and 3) pelts had a value of $50 each.

When I returned to the traps after school, I discovered the trapped raccoon had – as you might guess – chewed off his foot for his own survival. I was pissed and quickly developed new methods for harvesting trapped raccoons, and I'll leave those details out of this book. I will say that I'd become quite driven and determined to complete the task. My trap line grew to three total, and by the end of trapping season, I'd made $1,000.00. Plus, I'd saved our sweet corn patch and thinned the population to the benefit of other farmers in the area.

Where Do You Want to Go?

I realize this is an extreme example to underscore my points about drive and determination, but it does prove that when you set your mind to it, you can do anything.

Goal setting has always been a focus of mine every year. I actually still have hand-written goals from many years ago, and I enjoy reviewing them once in a while to get a clearer picture of my accomplishments and what I've done in my life.

It's simple: If you don't know where you want to go, you don't know how to get there. Or as the Cheshire Cat in Lewis Carroll's *Alice in Wonderland* phrased it so perfectly, "If you don't know where you're going, any road will take you there." Not knowing where you're going invariably leads to going in the wrong direction only to have to backtrack or worse, going around and around in circles. What a waste of time and energy.

> *Pick your destination and then plan your route. Without that, you're simply spinning your wheels.*

Your journey should lead you to your goal, and obviously, setting that goal is certainly step one. Getting there may be tough, but setting and achieving goals is the foundation of all achievement and success.

In managing IT projects, our goals were always written and measured according to set timeframes. They were also specific. We didn't simply say, "Go live." We delineated exactly what was going to go live, when, where, and who was both required for the work and as the beneficiary.

You've heard the term SMART goals: Specific, Measurable, Assignable, Realistic and Timely. What you can't say is, I want a million dollars. That doesn't mean you can't have a goal of achieving a million dollars. Yes, it's specific ($1,000,000), measurable (look at your bank account), and assignable (it's up to you). As for realistic, well, that's where the rubber meets the road and you have to determine your strategy and course of action to meet the goal and also set the timeframe for your target to achieve it. Wishing doesn't make it so. Strategy, planning, and action are the keys to success.

Reaching goals is certainly cause for celebration. More times than not, the big "wins" in project management did not come until the very end. That said, we did set milestones and have smaller wins as we progressed, but customer satisfaction really only occurred with the big win upon completion.

The same is true in real estate. The goal is to achieve financial success through real estate investing. Achieving that is the big win. However, there are smaller milestone wins that you can celebrate along the way: finding the right property, writing a viable and reasonable offer, offer acceptance, securing financing, completing the inspection, re-negotiating as needed, and proper appraisals. When you finally get to closing and receive the keys, go ahead and pop the cork!

Without leadership embracing and exhibiting drive and determination, any project could fail. It was my responsibility to keep the team motivated. Bumpy rides were expected, and oh yes, we encountered them. I lost many nights of sleep, but never lost my focus on drive and determination.

Keep pushing. The only way to get past it is to go through it.

Consider This...

Dana Linn Bailey, IFBB pro fitness and figure competitor believes:

If you have discipline, drive, and determination, nothing is impossible.

I like to think of it this way: When you have discipline (getting up early and always doing what needs to be done), drive (ability to pursue your dreams), and determination (ability to keep going) everything IS possible.

Chapter Ten:

"Let's Catch Up"

Here's where the story ends and how I landed upon the title of this book, *Why My J.O.B. Quit Me: Jump-start Your Firing,* all comes together and will make sense.

It was around 2009, and I was working for a large consulting firm, managing the two largest projects on the docket and traveling between two cities on a monthly basis. Workdays lasted 12 to 15 hours, I was coping with my father's death, and I was unaware that I was entering menopause. Doctors were "trying" various medications for me to feel and get healthy, and I learned that my body was unusual, having many adverse effects to the various meds prescribed and making my life worse. My fiancé and I had broken up; my house had been robbed; and I received the dreaded email invitation with the subject line: "Let's catch up."

You may interpret that invitation as little more than an opportunity to talk to your boss and review projects. Not me. I knew *exactly* what it meant. And I'm about to divulge publicly for the first time how I knew what "let's catch up" really meant. (To my ex-employer, if you're reading this, you'll now know how I figured it out.) But first, let me say that I thoroughly loved working for that consulting firm. I respected the principals and appreciated the lessons I learned and my co-workers. Life was good there, but….

I didn't fit in. And I didn't fit in because they didn't know what to do with me. When they asked if I wanted to be a director, I declined. They couldn't dangle the money carrot in front of me because I didn't want money. I simply wanted to run projects with no desire to climb the corporate ladder. At the time, I don't think I understood it myself. Others were suggesting I launch my own consulting business, something I'd never really thought about or considered.

However, I'd built up my real estate portfolio and was doing well in that arena. I knew it was a passion. Just because I felt I didn't fit in, I didn't know my employer also perceived it. But let's face it: you can only turn down so many promotions and money before something has to give. So there I was, working on-site on a Friday afternoon, when the "Let's catch up" invitation email hits. I immediately declined it; I knew what I was doing. Ten minutes later, he sent it back, now stating it was a mandatory meeting. Once again, I declined. Yup, I had the "balls" to do such a thing. Now I got a phone call. He was polite, but I could hear the urgency in his voice.

I accepted the meeting, but I first called his boss. When she answered, I asked directly: "Can you tell me why I'm getting fired on Monday?"

Her reply: "You're crazy. You're not getting fired." She was less than believable, and I knew she was lying.

You see, our consulting firm had well-defined processes, even when using email and the calendaring system. Everyone had access to everyone else's calendars. However, private meetings were marked as such so no one else could see the details. You could only see the duration but not the participants. I knew that another consultant had received the same "Let's catch up" invitation a few months prior, and the end result of that was his termination.

While I'd like to think I'm psychic, I'm not. I'm simply very observant and with a good memory. So I told my team I was getting fired on Monday. They didn't believe me, but when I walked into the meeting on Monday afternoon, I was fully prepared for my termination. There were some extenuating circumstances, and technically, I was never "fired." But we agreed to part ways.

It was a blessing! The pressures were immediately lifted and I felt nothing but relief. However, as I'd shared earlier what happened next set me back again: My best friend died of colon cancer. Talk about wanting to give up on life. I decided right then and there, I would take the next weeks off to clear my head and spend time with her husband and three kids. While on this hiatus, I had no worries at all. I knew there was a greater plan ahead for me; I just didn't know what it was exactly. I held on to that thought.

Once back home again, I learned that not having a J.O.B. would not pay bills and mortgages. My vision became clear and Project Strategixx LLC was born. I was back in business for myself and spent the next six months saving my home from foreclosure. As I shared, I successfully modified my loan and stayed in my house… all while building my new business.

My whole point in sharing my story, my upbringing, and my various career involvements is to emphasize to you that you too have your own set of skills that are allowing you (or will allow you) to become exactly who you want to become. My one regret is that I didn't learn my skills faster or more quickly embrace my own potential. If I had, I would have found myself where I wanted and was destined to be faster and at a much earlier age.

However, I embrace that I am right where I'm supposed to be now, marrying all of my life lesson skills with my project management skills along with my love for RVing and motorcycles.

Here's what I want you to really take away:

- Get quiet: Give your brain some quiet time and let it works its magic.
- Become fearless by learning to fear less.
- Remember that failure IS always an option. The road to success is often paved with that teacher, failure.
- Consider that every outcome you achieve is the result of the seeds you've planted. Choose seeds wisely and nurture them.
- Others' opinions should, nine times out of ten, be meaningless to you.
- Those who risk nothing, achieve nothing. Do you want to stay where you are or reach new heights? The choice is yours but does involve taking a risk.
- You need equal parts discipline and adaptability to succeed.
- It might be time to jump-start your own firing!

Stay tuned for my next book.

"Let's Catch Up"

Resources:

Suggested podcasts:

    Robert Kiyosaki:
    www.richdad.com/radio
    Darren Hardy:
    https://darrenhardy.com/darrendaily-on-demand
    Pastor Steven Furtick:
    elevationchurch.org/podcast/
    Pastor Rick Warren:
    pastorrick.com/listen/podcast/
    The Cashflow Guys:
    www.cashflowguys.com/podcast/
    Larry Harbolt
    http://www.larryharbolt.com/category/podcasts/

Maud Purcell, LCSW, CEAP, "The Health Benefits of Journaling."
https://psychcentral.com/lib/the-health-benefits-of-journaling/

For full articles regarding the round hay baler and additional photos, please visit:
https://mechielkopaska.com/fearless-book-resources/

Resources

About the Author

Mechiel Kopaska is, first and foremost, fearless. It's how she lives her life and runs her business.

She also thrives in environments that include countless moving parts and shifting landscapes which is why she exceled for so many years working as a project manager in the IT industry. It was the right combination of variety, change, and problem solving, but she saw that she was trading hours for money, and when she was fired (aka when her J.O.B. quit her), she was able to concentrate on her real estate investments full time, having been involved for more than a decade on a part-time basis.

Her success in real estate investing came through the school of hard knocks, but she focused on her vision, knowing she had what it took to learn, adapt, and create real freedom and true wealth for herself. At every turn, she connects with people and excels at solving their problems, and when she can't, she can find someone who can.

Mechiel has expanded her real estate business to now include hard money lending and developing RV parks. She also coaches others who are interested in mirroring her own success and finding the freedom, wealth, and satisfaction that she enjoys. As an innovative problem solver, she sees solutions that are either uncommon or difficult for others to find.

As Mechiel shares, "We all have people, situations, or things that bring up our insecurities and fears. Whether it's leaving the security of a job, being vulnerable with the people we love, or taking a risk on a new venture, we can always find something to worry about that will cause us to fear. But fear is just another thing that controls us, takes away our choices, and destroys our ability to thrive. Too many people let fear dictate their choices. Fear is a waste of time."

Connect with Mechiel at: www.fearlessinnovator.com

LinkedIn: www.linkedin.com/in/mechielkopaska/

Instagram:
https://www.instagram.com/fearlessinnovator44/

Or join her Facebook Group:
FEARLESS – Real Estate Innovator Group:
https://www.facebook.com/groups/1147527445623069/?ref=bookmarks